lots of pots

a girl said, "that man has lots of pots. hē has pots with tops. hē has pots with nō tops."

the man said, "I havₑ lots of cākₑs in pots. I havₑ a pot with a ship in it. I havₑ fish in pots."

1

the girl said, "can I have a pot fōr

a little fish?"

the man said, "this is a pot fōr a

little fish."

the girl said, "I will tāke this pot

hōme with mē." and shē did.

al and sal →

al said, "will wē gō hōme?" →

sal said, "nō. wē will gō to that farm." →

al said, "will wē have fun on that →

farm?" →

sal said, "wē can run with a cow. →

wē can ēat cōrn. wē can fēēd pigs. wē →

can sit in the lāke."

al said, "I hāte to sit in lākes."

sō sal and al did not sit in the lāke.

sal and al had fun with the pigs.

a fish in the rāin

ron met pat in the rāin. ron got wet.

pat got wet.

ron said, "this is not fun."

pat said, "this is fun."

ron said, "I havₑ wet fēēt. sō I

will gō hōmₑ. I do not nēēd rāin."

7

pat said, "wē can get fish."

sō shē got a fish and gāve it to him.

ron said, "it is fun to get wet if wē

get fish."

the pet shop

a girl said to a man, "let us gō to the

pet shop." sō the man and the girl went

down the rōad.

the man and the girl went in the pet

shop. the girl said to the man in the pet

shop, "I nēēd a dog."

the man said, "nō. I do not havₑ dogs.

I havₑ a red cat. let mē get that cat."

sō hē did. and the girl went hōmₑ with

the red cat.

the cow on the rōad

lots of men went in a little car. the

men went down a rōad.

a cow sat on the rōad. the cow did

not get up. sō the men ran to the cow.

the men said, "wē will lift this cow."

the men did not lift the cow. "this cow

is sō fat wē can not lift it."

the cow said, "I am not sō fat. I can lift mē." the cow went in the car.

the men said, "now wē can not get in the car." sō the men sat on the rōad and the cow went hōme in the car.

a girl and a gōat

a girl was on the rōad to a farm. shē met a gōat. shē said, "gō with mē to the farm. wē will pet a pig."

the gōat said, "I pet ducks and I pet chicks. I do not pet pigs."

the girl said, "it is fun to pet pigs.

pigs are fat."

the goat said, "I will not go to the farm. I will go to the park and pet a duck."

so the goat went to the park to pet a duck. and the girl went to the farm to pet a pig.

pāint that nōse

a fat dog met a little dog. the fat dog had a red nōse. the little dog had a red nōse.

the fat dog said, "I have a red nōse."

the little dog said, "I wish I did not have a red nōse."

the fat dog got a can of pāint. hē
said, "pāint that nōse."

sō the little dog did pāint his nōse. hē
said, "now this nōse is not red."

hē kissed the fat dog on the ēar. now
the fat dog has pāint on his ēar.

the red hat

the fish had a car and nō hat. shē said, "I do not nēēd a car. I nēēd a red hat."

shē met a cow. the cow had a red hat. the fish said, "can I have that red hat?"

the cow said, "nō."

the fish said, "I will give that cow a

car if she will let me have the hat."

the cow said, "take the hat and give

me a car." so the fish got a red hat

and the cow got a car.

a bug and a dog

a bug and a dog sat on a log. the

dog said, "that bug is sō littlе I can not

sēē him on the log."

the bug said, "I am big."

the dog said, "that bug on the log

is not big."

the bug said, "I will ēat this log."

and hē did. hē bit and bit and bit at the

log. the bug said, "now that dog can sēē

how big I am."

the dog said, "that bug can ēat logs

as well as a big bug can."

the bugs

a big bug met a little bug. the big bug

said, "let's gō ēat." sō the big bug āte a

lēaf and a nut and a rock. the big bug

said, "that is how big bugs ēat."

the little bug said, "now I will ēat."

sō the little bug āte a lēaf and a nut and

a rocₖ. then the littlₑ buᴳ went to a log

and biᴅ the log. ꜱhē āᴛₑ the log. then ꜱhē

āᴛₑ ten mōʀₑ logs.

"wow," the big buᴳ said. "that littlₑ

buᴳ can ēₐt a lot."

the littlₑ buᴳ said, "now let's ēₐt mōʀₑ."

the bug bus

a little bug sat on the back of a big dog. "get down," said the dog. "I am not a bus."

the bug did not get down. shē went to slēēp. the dog said, "I am not a bed."

the dog ran to the pond and went in.

the bug got wet. the bug said, "I am not a fish. tāke mē back to the sand."

"nō," the dog said.

sō the bug said, "I will get mōre bugs on this dog." ten bugs cāme and got on the dog.

the dog said, "I fēēl līke a bug bus."

and the dog went back to the sand with

the bugs.

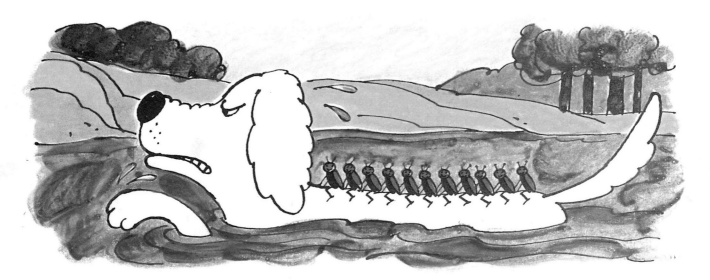

the man and his bed

a man had a tub. hē said, "I līke to

sit in the tub and rub, rub, rub."

then the man said, "now I will slēēp in

this bed." but a dog was in his bed.

the dog said, "can I slēēp in this bed?"

the man said, "nō. gō slēēp in the tub."

the dog said, "I līke to slēēp in beds."

the man said, "this dog līkes to slēēp

in beds. sō hē can slēēp with mē. but I

do not līke dogs that bīte."

the dog said, "I do not līke to bīte."

sō the man and the dog went to slēēp.

and the dog did not bīte the man.

the talking cat

the girl was gōīng fōr a walk. shē met
a fat cat. "can cats talk?" the girl said.

the cat said, "I can talk. but I do not
talk to girls. I talk to dogs."

the girl did not līke that cat. "I do
not līke cats that will not talk to mē."

the cat said, "I will not talk to girls."

the girl said, "I do not līke that cat.

and I do not give fish to cats I do not

līke."

the cat said, "I līke fish sō I will

talk to this girl." sō the girl and the cat

āte fish.

the dog that āte fish

a girl went fishiñg with a dog. that

dog āte fish. the girl did not līke the

dog to ēat fish. "do not ēat the fish," shē

said.

the girl went fishiñg and the dog went

to slēēp. the girl got fīve fish.

"give mē the fīve fish," the dog said.

"nō," the girl said. "mōre fish are in the lāke. dīve in and get them."

sō the dog went in the lāke. and the girl went to slēep.

the end

the rat got a sōre nōse

a rat and a rabbit went down a slīde.

the rabbit went down on his tāil. the

rat said, "I will gō down on the tāil."

the rat went up to the top of the slīde

and slid down on his nōse. hē said, "I

have a sōre nōse."

then hē said, "if a rabbit can gō down on his tāil, I will do the sāme." hē went up to the top. but hē cāme down on his nōse.

the rabbit said, "that rat can not tell if hē is on his nōse ōr his tāil."

the end

the rich pig →

a dog was in the park. it was dark in →

the park. →

shē ran into a pig. shē said, →

"pigs can not gō in this park. pigs live →

on farms." →

the pig said, "not this pig. I live on a →

ship. I am a rich pig."

the dog said, "tāke mē to the ship."

sō the pig did.

but the wāves māde the ship rock.

and the dog got sick.

the end

digging in the yard

a little man had a fat dog. the dog lived in the yard. the dog dug a hole in the yard. the little man got mad. "dogs can not dig in this yard. I will go for a cop." the dog dug and dug.

the man got a cop. the man said, "that

dog dug a big hōle in the yard."

the cop said, "dogs can not dig in

this yard."

the dog said, "I will stop. can I bē

a cop dog?"

the cop said, "yes. I nēēd a cop dog."

the end

ron said, "yes"

ron's dad tōld him to slēēp in bed.

"yes," ron said. and hē did.

his mom said, "ron, pāint this bed

red."

"yes," ron said. hē got the pāint and

māde the bed red.

"that is fīne," his mom said.

a big bōy met ron. hē said, "can ron pāint a car red?"

"yes," ron said. and hē māde the car red.

then ron went hōme. his mom said,

"ron māde a bed red and a car red. but

ron got lots of pāint on ron. ron is red."

sō ron went to the tub and went rub,

rub, rub. now ron is not red.

this is the end.

gōing to the park

a bōy met fīve girls. hē said, "let's gō to the park."

a girl said, "wē can not sēē the park. is the park nēar hēre?"

the bōy said, "nō. wē nēēd a car to get to the park."

the girls said, "wē do not havₑ a car."

the bōy said, "wē can not walk to the park. and wē can not rīdₑ to the park. how will wē get to the park?"

the girls said, "let's run." sō the bōy and the girls ran to the park.

this is the end.

hunting fōr a dēēr

ann said to her dad, "let's gō fīnd a dēēr fōr a pet."

sō ann and her dad went hunting fōr a dēēr. a dēēr cāme up to them. ann said, "you can bē a pet."

the dēēr said, "nō, a dēēr is not a pet.

dogs are pets. and cats are pets. I am
not a pet. but I will let a girl and her
dad pet mē."

the girl said, "that will bē fun." it was.

now, the girl has a pet dog and a pet
cat. they gō with her to hunt fōr the
dēēr that shē can pet.   the end

a card fōr mother

a bōy sent a card to his mother. the card said, "mother, I love you." but his mother did not get the card.

a cop got the card. shē said, "I am not mother." sō shē gāve the card to her brother.

her brother said, "this card is not

for mē. I am not mother."

so the cop and her brother went to

fīnd mother. they met the bōy.

the bōy said, "you have the card that

I sent to mother. give mē that card."

so they gāve him the card.

and hē gāve the card to his mother. →

this is the end. →